NANCY WATSON

Sadie, My Precious Blind Cat

Living With A Blind Cat Can Be Fun And Rewarding

First edition

This book was professionally typeset on Reedsy.
Find out more at reedsy.com

Contents

1

Introduction

This is a book about my blind cat Sadie. If you've never had a blind cat, it will show you that blind cats can be fun too. It will also help you be more comfortable in adopting one if the opportunity arises.

2

Looking for a New Cat

I've had cats growing up but I wasn't responsible for them – that was my Mom's job. When I graduated college and moved away from home for my new job in New Jersey, I became responsible myself. Up to now, I've had three cats as an adult. After my third cat Triton had to be put to sleep, I went looking for a new cat. Of course, I wanted to adopt a cat from a shelter. I like knowing that I've saved a cat and given them a forever home. I started my search online. One of the local shelters had a black and white cat available for adoption. I saw a picture of her and just fell in love with her. Then I found out that she was blind. I'll admit that I hesitated and thought about it for a few days. But her picture just kept drawing me back to her. Everyone was saying that I'd have to clean up my house (I'm a very messy person) and that I couldn't move any furniture around with a blind cat. But, in the end, I said YES! I filled out an application and then I had to go through an interview which I passed. She was born in September 2006 and she was about 3 years old when I adopted her.

3

Bringing Sadie Home

Sadie was being fostered by a person in Pennsylvania, so we met at someone's house half way between us. I went inside and the woman opened up her carrier and Sadie slowly walked out of it. She didn't seem to be afraid at all. I picked her up and put her in my carrier and drove home.

I prepared my laundry room so she would have a small room to stay in while she got used to the sounds of my house. She had a litter box, food, and water. I opened the carrier and she slowly walked out of it. I "showed" her where everything was and let her sniff and touch them. I was sitting on a stool and she came over and wanted petting. Whenever I pet her, her tail would whip from side to side. I kept stopping because it scared me and I thought she might bite me. After a while I realized she did that when she was excited.

I left her in the laundry room and went through the kitchen to my TV room. I sat down and was watching TV. I kept going back to visit her so she would know I hadn't abandoned her. That evening she started to really yell, enough that I opened the door. I went back to sit down in the TV room. She explored the kitchen first, then the TV room. She finally came to my recliner and I picked her up and put her on my lap.

An hour or so later, she jumped down and found her way back to the laundry room where she used the litter box. She then came back and laid on my lap. Then she did the same thing and ate some food and drank some water. It was then I knew I was right in adopting her.

That night, I left her in the laundry room and went to bed. But she started yelling again so I just let her out and went back to bed. Somehow she made it down the hallway to my bedroom. She couldn't jump onto my bed because it's too high but she could jump onto the laundry hamper at the foot of the bed and then get onto the bed. She doesn't seem to have any trouble jumping down from the bed.

She is so cute when she jumps down from something. She puts her stomach on the edge and reaches down as far as she can and then jumps the rest of the way.

Another thing I noticed when she was on my bed, when she walked around on the bed she would double tap her paws before putting full weight on them. She did this on anything unfamiliar.

4

Getting Used to the House

The next day, she explored the rest of the house. I moved her food and water into the kitchen. I noticed that when she drinks water, she puts her chin in the water as well. She'll also put her paw in the water – I guess to make sure there is water in the bowl. I can always tell when she has had water because of the water droplets on her chin and a wet paw. It's very cute.

I found that if she can reach the top of something, then she can jump up on it. She can't jump onto the counters because she can't reach the top of them. The same for the kitchen table. But she can jump onto the kitchen chairs and from there the kitchen table. So I still needed to train her not to get on the kitchen table. What I ended up doing was just shoving four of the chairs all the way under the table and putting stuff on the other two so she couldn't jump up on them. But she still managed to get up sometimes. Fortunately I didn't eat at the table (I ate on a TV tray in front of the TV) so I didn't mind. I had a lot of junk on the table and it was so cute when she would manage to get up on the table and climb on top of the junk and sit there like she conquered Mount Everest. But then I would have to help her get down again.

She even managed to jump up onto my recliner, onto the arm, and from there to the top of the back.

Then she explored my living room which also had a lot of junk in it. But she seemed to love climbing around on all of the junk.

She adjusted much better and quicker to the house than I expected. The junk didn't seem to faze her. If she bumped into something, she'd just figure out a way around it. She must have been born blind because she copes so well.

5

Life in New Jersey

I noticed that she always walks with a purpose – no hesitation. I lost electricity one time and it was totally dark. When I walked to get my flashlight, I walked slowly and put my hands in front of me so I wouldn't run into anything. I find it amazing that Sadie never did this. She always leads with her nose first!

Nothing seems to frighten her, not even thunderstorms or fireworks.

Whenever someone would come over and visit me, Sadie had to come and meet them. It turns out that Sadie likes people.

Sadie was able to figure out that she could jump onto the foot of my recliner when I was watching TV. I just had to move my feet out of her way. So I didn't have to keep picking her up.

At night Sadie would sleep with me. But she wants to sleep between my legs. I'm under the covers and she's on top of the covers. It certainly made it tough to turn over from side to side!

My other cats would always see my feet move when they're under the covers and pounce on them. But Sadie doesn't do that. The only time she'll play with my feet is if I poke her with a foot. And even then, she'll only bat at the foot a couple of times and lose interest if I keep my foot still.

Whenever I would come home, I'd take off my shoes and put on my house shoes. Sometimes, if Sadie stumbles across them, she would play with the laces of my shoes. Once she knew the shoes were there, she made it a point to play with the laces. I don't know how many times I've had to tie my shoes with wet laces.

Sadie loves to lick plastic and chew on paper. I don't know why, but after she vomits, she always seeks out plastic to lick. I had to keep her out of my office because she was always chewing on my papers.

I always keep the lid down on the toilet because my other cats always wanted to drink out of it. This was fortunate because Sadie managed to figure out how to jump onto the toilet and then from there onto the sink. She loved to lick the water droplets from the sink. Sometimes she would miss the sink and land in the waste basket, usually head first. Fortunately I was there to get her out. Sometimes she even jumps up when I'm brushing my teeth or washing my face and I have to hold her back. One time she wouldn't wait for me to put the lid down and she jumped up and fell in to the toilet – she gets very impatient and doesn't like to wait for me to finish.

I've found Sadie sitting in the hallway with her nose a half an inch from the wall. I don't think she knew how close to the wall she was. It was as if she was in a time out. It looked pretty funny watching her just sit there.

Going to the vet wasn't as difficult with Sadie as with my other cats. Whenever I would pull out the carrier, my other cats used to run and hide. I started pulling it out a week before we had to go to the vet. With Sadie being blind, I can pull it out whenever I want because she can't see me and she hasn't connected the zipper noise to the carrier. But she still doesn't like to go in the carrier.

I've taken a lot of pictures of her, but I've found that since she is blind her pupils are dilated and if she looks directly at the camera, I get glowing eyes. I keep those pictures anyway. I don't have the heart to delete them.

One year we had a hurricane hit the area and ever since then I've had an ant problem. But I kept it mostly under control. One day I got out of bed and went into the kitchen with Sadie following me. There was a pile of vomit on the floor with a ton of ants crawling all over it – I'm talking hundreds! I grabbed a napkin and started killing ants. Apparently dead crushed ants give off some sort of smell that Sadie loved. She rolled over onto her back and was wiggling away on top of them. I kept pushing her away to keep killing ants and she would keep coming back. I had a friend visiting at the time and all she could do was laugh. I'm laughing now but at the time I was just annoyed. I finally got a plastic bag and just scooped up the vomit and ants together and put it in the bag and then took it to the outside garbage can.

Sometimes I would leave the front door open and Sadie would love to sniff at the crack in the screen door. Her first Halloween, the kids would come and ring the doorbell and I'd open the door, give them candy, then close the door. I turned around and Sadie was walking towards the door. By the time Sadie hears the door open, realizes what it was and decides to come investigate, it's too late. This was very different from my other cats. One year Triton got out three times during Halloween and I would have to quickly go out and grab him. I felt bad closing the door before Sadie got to it, so I started leaving the door open with just the screen door closed and she would sit there sniffing. When the kids would come and ring the doorbell, I'd have to pick up Sadie before opening the door to give them candy. All of the kids loved seeing her and some even wanted to pet her. Sadie took it very well.

6

Playing with Sadie

Playing with Sadie was a challenge. I had one of those fishing rods with a toy on the end of the string that you cast out and reel back in that my other cats loved.But Sadie couldn't tell it was there unless I reeled it in and it touched her body. I had a feather boa on the end of a stick but I would have to stand close to her and touch her with the boa. She wasn't a fan of that. Then I thought about those plastic balls with the bell in the center. So I bought a container and she would play with them.She would bite one and carry it around in her mouth. Then she would drop it and bat at it. Then the hunt was on to find it. Most of the time she would find it. Some days, when I was very energetic, I would play soccer with her and the ball. But I was always stepping on the balls and they would break. So I went back to the store and found some foam balls. I bought a container of them. She loved those as well even though they didn't make any sound. They were easier to carry around in her mouth. And when I stepped on one, it just bounced back into shape. The benefit of these balls is that after she's played with them a while, they would have her scent on them so they were easier to find. But they would still get lost and I would have to keep buying more balls.

I've had cats that would get in a very frisky mood and zoom around the house. Since Sadie can't see, she doesn't do that. Instead, she frantically tries to jump up onto things that aren't there. One time, she jumped up in front of my recliner and landed on my chest. I learned after that to stand up when she gets in those moods.

7

The Sounds of Sadie

Sadie is not a quiet cat. Whenever I unexpectedly touch her, she makes noises. Whether it's a murmur, trill, warble, or meow, she lets me know she is aware of me. Even when I walk by her when she's awake and sitting on the floor, she makes noises. I guess she can feel the vibrations as I walk by. She has an especially loud and unique yell when it comes to her balls. When she finds her ball, she likes to sit on it and yell. When she loses her ball, it's the same yell. So, no matter where I am in the house, I know she either found a ball or lost a ball.

Sadie loves to be petted. No matter where I am! She purrs but it isn't loud which surprised me since she can meow so loud. She especially loves it when I'm sitting on the toilet. She will sit up on her hind legs like a gopher. The first time she did this, I was petting her and thinking how cute she was when she leaned backwards and pushed her head into my hand. She was a little too far away and my hand slipped and she fell over backwards. I was much more careful after that! But it still occasionally happens.

Sometimes she just sits in the middle of a room or on the bed and just meows very loud. She'll even sit next to my head while I'm in bed and scream in my ear. She does this for a minute or so, then they get quieter and then they stop. I don't know why. It doesn't matter if I'm there or not. I've even talked to her and that doesn't seem to quiet her down.

8

Cone Collar

In September 2017 Sadie had a growth removed from her back foot. The Vet said everything went fine except she didn't start breathing on her own afterwards until she started waking up. So they had to keep bagging her until she woke up. It scared my Vet – she's never had that happen before.

I knew she was going to have to have a cone collar when I brought her home so I went to the pet store before picking her up. I found one of those donut blow up collars and I got that thinking she would be able to eat and drink better with that type of collar.

I got her home and put the collar on her. But she was able to reach her back foot.

So I went back to the pet store and bought a small cone collar and put it on her.

It took her a while to get used to it. She could maneuver it enough to reach her food bowl. The water bowl was a different matter! I had to mop up the water quite often. If I was there I would hold the bowl in place for her. She also managed to get into the litter box and do her business okay. She would jump up into my lap for some loving. She likes putting her face close to my face and the cone would hit me so I had to be careful.

All in all, she managed very well wearing the cone collar. But she was certainly glad when I took it off.

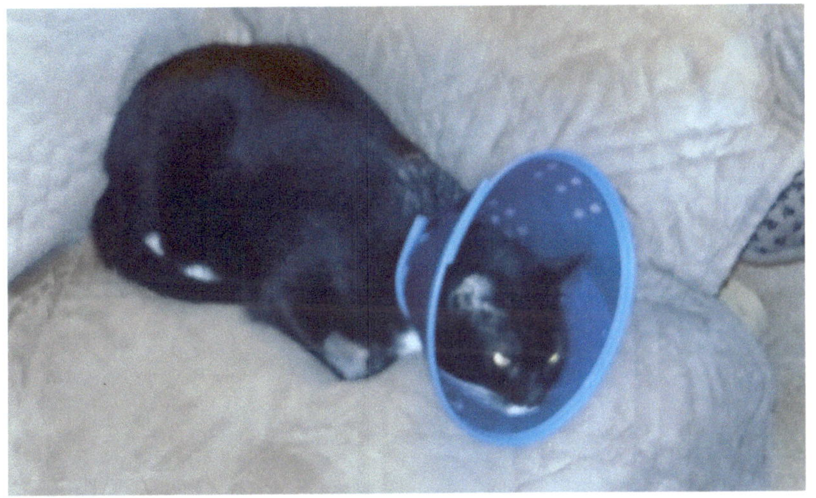

9

Moving to Tennessee

My parents were getting older and needed my help. I had enough years with the company I worked for to retire and collect a pension so I decided to sell my house in New Jersey and move back down to Tennessee. This was in November 2017.

Up to now, Sadie had no interest in the door from the laundry room into the garage. But then I was putting a lot of stuff in the garage ready for donations or the junk yard. One day I went into the garage and left the door open. After a few minutes I turned around and saw Sadie at the top step and, before I could get to her, she stepped/fell down to the next step. After that, I couldn't go into the garage without closing the door behind me. But she still sometimes managed to sneak in behind me.

I didn't look forward to the drive down with Sadie. I did that before when I drove up to New Jersey and my cat at that time didn't take it very well. But when I went home on vacation, I took that same cat on the plane with me and she did great. Plus I wasn't closing on my house until January 31, 2018 and I didn't want her to get agitated when the movers were packing and loading up the truck. So I decided to fly Sadie down with me when I went home for Christmas vacation and leave her with my parents when I flew back the beginning of January.

When we got to my parents' house, I tried to keep her closed off from most of the house. She had the run of my bedroom, bathroom, and the other bedroom where her food, water, and litter box are. But, again, she insisted on getting out of that part of the house and into the den, kitchen, home office, and living/dining rooms. She could only be in the living/dining rooms when I was in there because there was carpeting on the floor and she has a habit of throwing up once in a while.

When I went to bed, I would close off our area from the rest of the house. I had to stack two boxes, one taller and one shorter, side by side like stairs and put them at the foot of my bed so she could get on the bed without any trouble. She adjusted very well to her new living conditions.

She even figured out how to jump from the toilet to the sink counter. I don't know how because I have to close the door at my parent's house so she wasn't in the bathroom when I flushed the toilet and washed my hands. She also gets into the bathtub (I had a shower stall in New Jersey) to lick up the water droplets.

My Mom has a chair next to a table where her "filing cabinet" is. That's where she opens the mail and puts the important papers leaning up against the table lamp. Sadie figured out how to jump onto the chair, then onto the table, and then started chewing on her paperwork. I don't know how many times we had to pick her up and put her on the floor.

At Christmas, we had decorated an artificial tree in the living room. Sadie would do her roaming in the living room and bump into the ornaments on the bottom limbs. She would bat at them a few times and then walk away. Thankfully, she had no interest in climbing the tree! Fortunately she didn't chew on the paper wrapped presents we then put under the tree.

Then I left to go back to New Jersey to close on my house.

I kept asking my Mom on the phone how Sadie was doing and she said fine. It turns out that Sadie didn't like being shut up in that part of the house by herself, so my Mom just opened up the door and let her roam around the house except she kept the door to the dining/living rooms closed. My Mom had the chore of giving Sadie food and water and cleaning the litter box. My Dad had the joy of Sadie laying on his lap when he was sitting in his recliner. And that is exactly where she was when I drove up and walked into the house. She was glad to hear my voice and she jumped down and came over to me for some loving.

Mom told me that one morning Sadie wasn't around so she went looking for her. Mom found her laying in the carrier. I had left it open when I went back to New Jersey. Another time, there was a thunderstorm at night and when Mom got up in the morning Sadie wasn't around. Mom went looking for her and found her sleeping in my Dad's office under one of the tables on top of a box. She still occasionally likes to sleep there.

The packers came and packed up all my stuff. Then the movers came and took out all of the boxes first. Then they took out all of the furniture. They must have unearthed about 50 balls and asked me if I had a pet. I said yes but she was already down in Tennessee. I always had to buy new balls and wondered where all of the balls went. Now I know.

10

Life in my Parents' House

Sadie would sleep with me on my bed every night at the beginning. She would continue to want to lay in my Dad's lap. He would reach down and pet her but he wouldn't pick her up. I think he thought his job was done. Then he started reading books on his tablet and get so involved that he wouldn't even realize she was sitting there waiting. It was so sad for me to see her just sitting on the floor between his feet. She would wait five or ten minutes and then leave. I would pick her up and set her down next to me on the sofa and she would lay there content.

Then, after about six months, she started sleeping in the den at night. I was so used to her sleeping with me that I really missed her. But you can't make a cat stay with you. So I just let her be.

My parents had to get used to Sadie wondering around and being underfoot. She really liked to come and sit behind anyone especially in the kitchen. So Mom learned not to back up without looking first. But we still had to be careful when we're walking around and have to get around Sadie when she is in her roaming mood. She is notorious for going in the opposite direction from where you think she's going to go.

Mom likes to leave the back door and storm door open to make it easier to bring in the groceries. One day Sadie must have followed Mom out because when Mom started back in with some groceries, Sadie had gotten down the three steps and was sitting on the carport. Fortunately she didn't run any further and my Mom was able to get her back into the house. So now we have to shut her up in our side of the house so she can't get outside when Mom brings in the groceries.

Then she would sometimes sleep with me and sometimes sleep in the den. We all settled into a routine. I would sometimes watch a ball game with my Dad in the den, and other times I would watch my shows on the TV in the living room – sometimes with my Mom. My Dad only liked sports. No matter which room I'm in, Sadie will find me.

Now, she sleeps most nights with me. Sometimes she sleeps next to my pillow, sometimes at my feet, and sometimes she wants to sleep between my legs like she used to.

In the morning, when Sadie thinks I should get up, she walks all around me on the bed (including walking across the top of my pillow) and then yells in my ear. She will do this multiple times until I either get up or she gives up on me.

Mom keeps a small stool in the kitchen. She keeps it under the bar and Sadie likes to sit on it and just yell.

Of course, we had to train Sadie not to get on the dining room table. The chairs at my parent's house don't go all the way under the table. So Sadie would jump up on the chairs and then the table. I would tell her NO and then take her off the table and put her on the floor. It took a few months but she only gets on the table once in a blue moon now.

We ended up having to keep Sadie out of the dining room while we were eating. My parents drop food on the rug and Sadie would find it and eat it. Then, sometimes, she would throw up. She still wants to be in the dining room. Most days we hear her bumping into the door because she wants in. So we keep her out until I can pick up the food from the rug. Then I open the door. Sadie comes in searching for food. When she doesn't find any, she walks out.

11

My Nephew's Daughter

Every week my Mom would cook dinner and invite my brother, my nephew and his wife. They would arrive and sit on the sofa in the den. Sadie would come over and sniff their shoes. Then she would play with the laces. She would even untie their shoe laces. The first time my nephew didn't notice until he got up and started walking. Then they came to expect it. She was so cute doing it that we didn't stop her. Sometimes when company would take their sneakers off, Sadie would stick her head down the shoe as far as it would go. I guess she loves the smell of sweaty/stinky sneakers.

After a couple of months, my nephew and his wife had their first child, a baby girl. They would bring her to the weekly dinners as well. After dinner, we would all move into the living room and watch the baby. Sadie would be there as well and would sniff the baby. Once the baby could turn over, they would but a blanket down and place her on it. And we would watch her. Sadie was there as well. Then when the baby could crawl, she noticed Sadie and would try to grab her around the neck. Sadie just sat there and took it. She never swiped or tried to bite the baby. And I made sure that the baby never hurt Sadie. I was so surprised how well Sadie interacted with the baby. Sadie must have been around babies before I adopted her. After several months of watching Sadie interact with the baby, all at once it changed. The baby started to walk and Sadie started running away and hiding

Now, my nephew and his wife have another baby girl. When both children come over, Sadie runs away. I'm hoping when the kids are older they'll be able to play with Sadie.

12

This Year

The beginning of February we had a massive ice storm that knocked out our power for a week. We managed the first night okay, but it just got too cold for us. Fortunately my sister's electricity came back on the second day. So, Mom, Sadie, and I packed our things and went and stayed at her house. She gave me the upstairs bedroom because it had a private bathroom. I set up Sadie's food, water, and litter box in the bathroom. I kept Sadie up there for a couple of days. I found it interesting that she didn't want to jump onto the bed or the futon sofa next to the bed. She liked laying on the rug in the bathroom. One evening, I opened the door to go downstairs and Sadie was finally curious about what was beyond the door. So I let her out and she walked forward. Of course, when she got to the top stair, she fell down to the next stair. But then she slowly made her way down the stairs and stopped at the bottom of the stairs. I decided that was far enough for that day and put her back in the bedroom. My thought was to introduce her to my sister's cat the next day. But first, I had to take her to the vet to get her annual shots. Plus her skin condition seemed to be much worse – she has miliary dermatitis. It turns out that she had fleas and that made the skin condition much worse. I was shocked she had fleas. My Mom must have brought some fleas in after working in the yard. The vet said that even with the cold weather and ice storm, it wasn't enough to kill the fleas outside. So they gave her an antibiotic and steroid shots along with her annual shots plus some monthly topical flea treatment. So I took her back to my sister's house and left her in my bedroom. I won't be letting her out into the rest of the house. I certainly didn't want the fleas to spread beyond the bedroom.

So then I had to flea bomb my Mom's house before we could move back in. But when we finally moved back in to my Mom's house, Sadie was so happy to be back.

We've all settled into a routine and Sadie is happy. Mom has gotten used to her being underfoot. My Dad, unfortunately, passed away earlier this year. Sadie is getting older now (16 years old this year) so she sleeps more and plays less.

13

Conclusion

I really hope you've enjoyed reading about Sadie as much as I've enjoyed writing about her! And that it has helped you realize that blind cats can be fun and rewarding to adopt and you won't hesitate if the opportunity arises.

If you found this book helpful, I'd be very appreciative if you left a favorable review for the book on Amazon!

www.ingramcontent.com/pod-product-compliance
Lightning Source LLC
LaVergne TN
LVHW021351160826
845679LV00008B/1572

* 9 7 9 8 8 4 7 1 0 1 1 9 6 *